The Erie Canal

by Andrew Santella

Content Adviser: Andrew P. Kitzmann,
Assistant Director/Curator, Erie Canal Museum,
Syracuse, New York

Reading Adviser: Rosemary G. Palmer, Ph.D.,
Department of Literacy, College of Education,
Boise State University

COMPASS POINT BOOKS
MINNEAPOLIS, MINNESOTA

Compass Point Books
3109 West 50th Street, #115
Minneapolis, MN 55410

Visit Compass Point Books on the Internet at *www.compasspointbooks.com*
or e-mail your request to *custserv@compasspointbooks.com*

On the cover: The Erie Canal

Photographs ©: Bettmann/Corbis, cover, 34; North Wind Picture Archives, 5, 7, 17, 19, 21, 22, 23, 35, 37, 38; William Manning/Corbis, 8; David Muench/Corbis, 9; Courtesy of Brauer Museum of Art, 10; Image courtesy Erie Canal Museum, Syracuse, N.Y., www.eriecanalmuseum.org, 11, 15, 25, 28, 36, 39; Alan Schein Photography/Corbis, 12; Corbis, 13, 30; Hulton/Archive by Getty Images, 16, 27; Rochester Images: Rochester Public Library Local History Collection, 24; Lee Snider/Corbis, 29, 41; Library of Congress, 32; Courtesy of New York State Thruway, 33; Express Newspapers/Getty Images, 40.

Creative Director: Terri Foley
Managing Editor: Catherine Neitge
Photo Researcher: Marcie C. Spence
Designer/Page production: Bradfordesign, Inc./Jaime Martens
Cartographer: XNR Productions, Inc.

Library of Congress Cataloging-in-Publication Data
Santella, Andrew.
The Erie Canal / by Andrew Santella.
    p. cm. — (We the people)
  Includes bibliographical references and index.
  ISBN 0-7565-0679-4 (hardcover)
  1. Erie Canal (N.Y.)—History—Juvenile literature. [1. Erie Canal (N.Y.)] I. Title. II. We the
people (Series) (Compass Point Books)
  HE396.E6S26 2005
  386'.48'09747—dc22   2003024175

TABLE OF CONTENTS

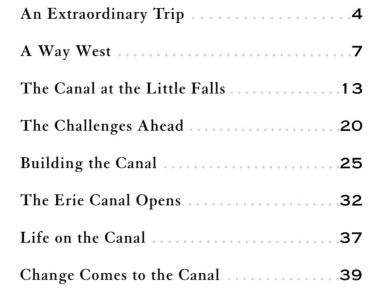

NOTE: *In this book, words that are defined in the glossary are in* **bold** *the first time they appear in the text.*

An Extraordinary Trip

On October 26, 1825, a boat called the *Seneca Chief* set out from Buffalo, New York, on a 500-mile (800-kilometer) journey. This was to be no ordinary trip. The *Seneca Chief* was the first boat to travel the full length of the Erie Canal.

The Erie Canal was a manmade waterway that stretched 363 miles (581 kilometers) across the state of New York from Lake Erie to the Hudson River. It was one of the greatest building projects of the early United States. Using little more than shovels and their own muscle power, thousands of workers dug a ditch 40 feet (12 meters) wide that would become the canal. They built bridges and other structures that still stand today. It took them eight long years to complete the canal, but their work changed the face of the United States.

The canal provided the first important link between the Atlantic Ocean and the Great Lakes.

4

The Seneca Chief *was the first boat to travel the full length of the Erie Canal.*

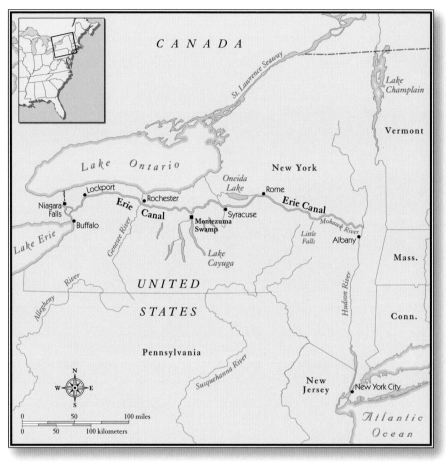

A map of the Erie Canal

It encouraged trade between the cities of the Atlantic **seaboard** and the growing states of the Midwest. It helped make New York City the business center of the United States. And it helped thousands of settlers make their way west to start new lives.

6

A WAY WEST

At the start of the 1800s, most Americans lived along the Atlantic seaboard, a narrow stretch of land on the East Coast. The heartland of the American Midwest beckoned, however. Great tracts of land there held fertile soil for farming plus minerals and other natural resources for industry use.

Most Americans lived along the coast of the Atlantic Ocean.

One thing stood in the way. The Appalachian Mountains stretched from Maine to Georgia, forming a barrier to westward movement. Few roads cut through the mountains. The ones that did lead west were full of holes and ruts that damaged wagon wheels and made travel difficult. In the winter, snow and rain turned the roads muddy and made them almost impossible to use.

Travel by river offered another alternative. In fact, in the early 1800s, travel by water was usually faster and

8

The Appalachian Mountains stood in the way of western travel.

The Mohawk River stretches across New York.

easier than traveling over roads. The problem was that
only a few rivers cut through the Appalachian Mountains.
One of these was the Mohawk River of New York. By the
start of the 1800s, settlers had already made their way west
along the Mohawk and established towns on its banks.
However, waterfalls and **rapids** stood in the way of boats
trying to make their way west on the Mohawk. What
was needed was an easier and faster way for people and
products to travel between the eastern United States and
the Great Lakes region.

9

One solution was to build a canal. A canal is a human-made waterway that connects natural bodies of water and allows boats to travel in places they couldn't before. People had long considered building a canal to connect Lake Erie and the Hudson River. In fact, the idea had been suggested as far back as the early 1700s, before the United States won its independence from Great Britain. Such a canal would allow people and products to travel by water from the Atlantic Ocean deep into the heartland of North America. Timber, farm produce, and minerals all would flow from the heartland to the big cities of the East.

A canal from Lake Erie, painted here at sunset, was under consideration for many years.

The Erie Canal today at Dewitt, New York

In 1784, an Irish engineer named Christopher Colles presented a plan for a canal to the New York state Legislature. Colles's plan called for building a canal along the Mohawk River from Albany to Lake Erie. The Legislature was not ready to take on such an ambitious project. However, some leading New Yorkers liked his plan and began to take steps to turn the plan into a reality. One of the first steps was the formation of two private companies devoted to the building of canals and **locks.**

11

The Hudson River, shown here at the Bear Mountain Bridge, has always been a key waterway.

In 1792, the Western Inland Lock Navigation
Company was formed with the goal of opening a waterway between the Hudson River and Great Lakes to the
west. That same year, the Northern Inland Lock Navigation
Company was formed. Its goal was to improve navigation
between the Hudson River and Lake Champlain to the north.

THE CANAL AT
THE LITTLE FALLS

The Western Inland Lock Navigation Company was the
first to actually begin digging a canal. In 1793, the
company began work on a small canal around the Little
Falls of the Mohawk River. These waterfalls blocked boats

The canal at the Little Falls

13

traveling down the Mohawk. Riverboats loaded with goods had to stop when they came to the Little Falls. All their **cargo** had to be unloaded and carried around the waterfalls, sometimes along with the boat itself. This procedure is called a portage.

The new canal changed all this. It was only a mile long, but it made a huge difference to the farmers and businesspeople who shipped their goods on the Mohawk River. For the first time, riverboats could move around the Little Falls without stopping and unloading.

To complete the canal, builders had to construct a series of locks. A lock consists of an enclosed section of the canal with gates on either end. A boat enters the lock through a gate and is shut inside the lock. Then a **sluice** is opened in one of the gates, allowing water to enter the lock. As water enters, the water level rises, and the boat rises with it. When the boat reaches the desired level, the other gate is opened and the boat moves on. The locks built at the Little Falls were the first in the United States.

14

A canal boat enters the lock at Durhamville, New York.

The canal at the Little Falls allowed boats to travel the Mohawk River more quickly and easily. It helped farmers and businesspeople save time and money, and it convinced other people to build more canals. In 1797, inventor Robert Fulton wrote a letter to President George Washington about the possibility of building a long canal in New York state. No further building was done, however. Then in 1807 and 1808, a merchant from western New York named Jesse Hawley wrote newspaper articles in the

Robert Fulton

Genesee *Messenger* urging the state of New York to build a canal connecting the Hudson River and Lake Erie.

Finally, the New York state Legislature acted. In 1808, the Legislature ordered a survey of the various routes

16

that such a canal might follow. The survey was led by Judge James Geddes, who eventually walked much of the distance. Still, little was done to begin construction of this huge project. No one seemed to know who would pay for the canal or how it could be built.

James Geddes

In fact, the Erie Canal might never have been completed without the efforts of one influential New York politician. De Witt Clinton had served in the state Legislature and was mayor of New York City. He believed a long canal would spark the growth and prosperity of New York City and the rest of New York state.

Not everyone agreed with Clinton. To many people, the idea of building such a long and costly canal seemed foolish. Much of western New York was covered with thick forests and swamps. Workers would have to dig, scrape, and build nearly 400 miles (640 kilometers) of canal.

Most important, few people agreed on who would pay for building the canal. Some New Yorkers hoped the federal government would pay for it. President Thomas Jefferson, however, did not agree. He called Clinton's plan "little short of madness." Others called the proposed canal Clinton's Folly or Clinton's Ditch.

In 1817, however, Clinton was elected governor of New York. He convinced the New York state Legislature to provide $7 million for a new canal. Clinton's Ditch would be built after all.

De Witt Clinton led the movement to build the Erie Canal.

19

THE CHALLENGES AHEAD

Nothing like the Erie Canal had ever been built in the United States. Up until then, the country's longest canal was just 27 miles (43 kilometers) long. The Erie Canal would stretch for 363 miles (581 kilometers). It would measure 40 feet (12 meters) wide and 4 feet (1.2 meters) deep. Alongside the canal would be a walking path for mules and horses called a towpath. Boats on the canal would be pulled along by these animals instead of driven by engines or wind power.

The canal was built without any of the motorized equipment that is used in construction today. The workers who built the Erie Canal had no bulldozers or jackhammers or trucks. They dug with plows and shovels. They carted heavy stone in wagons pulled by mules. When they needed to cut through solid rock, they blasted it with gunpowder.

In 1817, there were very few engineers in the United States with any experience in designing canals. In fact, not a

The Erie Canal at Schenectady, New York

single school of engineering existed in the country at the time. The builders of the Erie Canal had to learn as they worked. Some of the engineers in charge of building the canal looked to England for expert help. English engineers had been designing and building canals for many years. New Yorkers traveled to England to observe how canals there worked.

They took notes and made drawings of the canals. An English engineer named William Weston agreed to provide expert help to the planners of the Erie Canal. His assistant, Benjamin Wright, later became chief engineer of the canal.

Benjamin Wright

It wasn't simply the length of the canal that made it such a challenging project. The canal's builders also had to overcome natural obstacles like mountains, swamps, and rivers. The canal would travel through hilly and uneven country, but planners wanted the canal to be perfectly flat and level. A flat and level canal would be easier to maintain, and it would mean that boats would not have to make any difficult uphill climbs.

22

A series of five locks carried boats up the steep incline at Lockport.

The land of New York state was anything but flat and level, however. Lake Erie sits more than 550 feet (168 meters) higher than the Hudson River at Albany. To raise and lower boats, builders had to construct 83 locks along the length of the canal. Each lock could raise or lower boats 6 to 12 feet (1.8 to 3.6 meters). In some places, a series of locks was built to raise and lower boats as much as 66 feet (20 meters). At Lockport in western New York, builders designed a series of five locks that carried boats up a steep rise called the Niagara **Escarpment.** This was the only place on the original canal that had double locks.

Engineers also had to find ways to build the canal over swamps, valleys, and rivers. Their solution was to build aqueducts, which are raised structures like bridges that carry water over an obstacle. Just like modern high-ways sometimes pass over other highways, aqueducts allowed canals to pass over rivers and streams. The aqueduct over the Genesee River in Rochester extended 802 feet (245 meters).

The aqueduct over the Genesee River in Rochester in the late 1800s.

BUILDING THE CANAL

On July 4, 1817, a crowd gathered in Rome, New York, to see construction begin. The event was celebrated with speeches and the firing of cannons. Rome was a small town about halfway between the Hudson River and Lake Erie. Construction was started there because the land in the area was flat and easy to travel. Construction crews could head west for 80 miles (128 kilometers) before they had to build a single lock or aqueduct.

A bridge crosses the Erie Canal at Dewitt.

25

Still, construction of the canal was a slow and difficult process. First, surveyors measured a path 60 feet (18 meters) wide for the canal to follow. This path allowed enough room for the canal, the **berm,** and the towpath. Next, the canal's path had to be made completely straight and level. Trees had to be cut down and stumps dug up. Dips in the path were filled in and small hills knocked down. In some places, workers used hammers and chisels to chip away at rock that blocked the path of the canal. In other places, they used gunpowder to blast open a path. Not surprisingly, this practice proved to be a dangerous one, and many workers were injured in blasting accidents. All these preparations had to be completed before workers could even begin digging the canal itself.

Because no construction project of this kind had ever been attempted, workers often had to invent new devices to help them do their jobs. For example, they had to cut down so many trees in the thick forests of New York that work was often delayed waiting for trees to be removed.

Thick forests border the Genesee River in this 1859 photo.

27

An old drawing shows the huge spool used to pull up tree trunks.

So workers developed a method for cutting down trees that was faster than using axes. They attached cables high in the large, old trees. The cables were hooked to a huge roller that was turned by a crank, and the tree was simply pulled down.

To pull up tree stumps, the canal builders developed yet another new method. They wrapped a chain around the stump and attached the chain to an enormous spool about 14 feet (4 meters) across. Then, a team of mules or oxen pulled on cable that made the spool go around.

As the spool spun around, the chain tightened and eventually pulled the stump up. This new method proved much faster and easier than the old ways of removing stumps, which involved burning them and chopping them with axes.

Building the aqueducts and locks required new methods as well. Most were made of blocks of stone held

The bridge and aqueducts at Fort Hunter were built in 1839.

29

together by cement. One challenge for engineers was to find cement that would work underwater. An engineer named Canvass White discovered a source of limestone that he could make into cement that dried quickly and held fast even underwater.

Workers operate a manual pulley crane during the building of the canal near Lockport.

The workers who built the canal came from the farms of New York state and from big cities such as Boston and New York City. Many were immigrants who had recently arrived from Ireland and other countries. They worked long, hard hours but were paid just $8 to $12 a month, or 50 cents a day.

Their working conditions were often miserable. In the Montezuma Swamp west of Syracuse, workers often had to slog through mud that came up to their knees or higher. Under such awful conditions, workers easily fell ill.

No one knows exactly how many workers lost their lives, but many died of malaria, pneumonia, and other illnesses. They were often buried in unmarked graves along the canal.

THE ERIE CANAL OPENS

A small section of the canal opened to boat traffic in 1819. Construction continued on the canal for eight years before it was completed. Finally in 1825, Governor Clinton of New York climbed onboard the *Seneca Chief* in Buffalo to officially open the canal. Cannons placed along the entire canal were fired to mark its opening. One after another they boomed, until news of the opening had reached from one end of the canal to the other. It took one hour and 20 minutes from when the first cannon was fired until the last was fired.

Governor De Witt Clinton and guests take the first boat trip on the Erie Canal.

A mural painted in 1905 by C.Y. Turner at DeWitt Clinton High School in the Bronx celebrates the linking of Lake Erie and the Atlantic Ocean.

The *Seneca Chief* traveled the length of the canal from Buffalo to Albany. From there, it headed south down the Hudson River, bound for New York City and the Atlantic Ocean. Clinton carried with him kegs of water from Lake Erie. When the *Seneca Chief* reached the ocean, Clinton poured the water from the lake into the ocean to celebrate the Erie Canal's linking of the two great bodies of water.

Farmers and businesses could now ship goods quickly by boat.

The Erie Canal made travel much faster. The *Seneca Chief* made it from Buffalo to Albany in 10 days. An overland trip might have taken two or three weeks. Trade boomed, as farms and businesses used the canal to ship goods. From the Midwest came wheat, coal, lumber, iron, and salt, all bound for the big cities of the East. Factories in New York City used the canal to send manufactured goods to farms and small towns in western New York and beyond.

The canal helped make New York City the busiest port in the United States. Before the canal was completed, New York had been the fifth-busiest port in the country. Soon, however, more goods were being shipped through New York than through Boston, Baltimore, and New Orleans combined. Other cities along the canal prospered as well. Syracuse grew from a small town of 250 people to a city of 22,000 between 1820 and 1850. Today, much of the population of New York state lives along the canal route.

Erie Canal boats would tie up in New York City.

Farms prospered along the Erie Canal.

Canal boats also carried people to the open lands of the Midwest. When the canal opened in 1825, it helped spur a great westward migration. Settlers traveled on canal boats to Lake Erie and then made their way west through the Great Lakes to Ohio, Illinois, and other states. Between 1820 and 1850, the populations of Ohio, Illinois, Indiana, and Michigan grew from fewer than 800,000 to more than 4 million.

The success of the Erie Canal encouraged the building of more canals. Several branch canals were added to the Erie Canal, connecting it to other bodies of water, such as Lake Ontario and Cayuga Lake.

LIFE ON THE CANAL

By 1845, thousands of boats traveled up and down the canal. In some places, traffic was so heavy that boats lined up to wait their turn to go through the locks. There were **packet boats** that carried passengers and boats that carried freight. Even circus boats went up and down the canal, carrying animals that put on shows in the towns along the way.

One of the most important jobs on the canal was performed by boys as young as 8 years old. They were called hoggees, and they drove the mules that walked on

Passengers enjoy a ride on the canal in the 1820s.

37

Hoggees drove the mules that pulled the boats in the Erie Canal.

the towpath pulling the boats by a rope. Each hoggee had to walk miles along the canal for up to six hours at a time. They also fed and cared for the animals, and they earned just $7 to $10 a month.

Many canal boats were owned and operated by families who made their homes on the boats. They slept in the cabin of the boat. Some boats even had spare room for mules or other work animals. Mothers and daughters cooked and helped take care of the boats. Fathers and sons operated the boats, handled work animals, and loaded and unloaded cargo.

CHANGE COMES TO THE CANAL

The Erie Canal was used so heavily that after 1835, it was improved to handle more traffic. It was enlarged from 4 feet (1.2 meters) deep to 7 feet (2 meters) deep so that larger boats could use the canal.

In 1905, it was enlarged again. This time, engineers abandoned parts of the original canal and instead widened and deepened natural riverbeds. Workers dug new channels

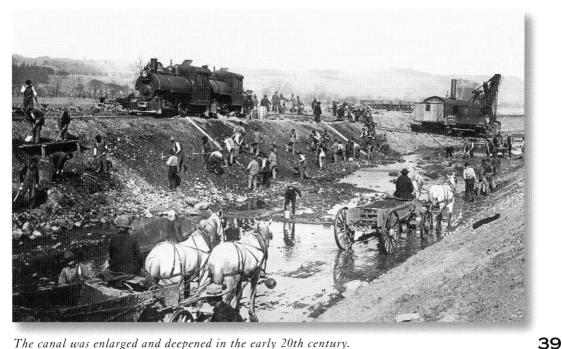

The canal was enlarged and deepened in the early 20th century.

39

as deep as 14 feet (4.2 meters) to handle canal traffic, then filled in parts of the original canal. Completed in 1918, the new canal was named the New York State Barge Canal. That canal, which includes parts of the original Erie Canal, still exists today.

However, by the 1950s, traffic on the canal had slowed. Railroads moved passengers and products more quickly. So did modern highways. In 1959, the St. Lawrence Seaway opened in Canada, creating another water connection between the Atlantic Ocean and the Great Lakes. The seaway was deep enough and wide enough to handle the largest oceangoing ships.

U.S. President Dwight D. Eisenhower, and Great Britain's Queen Elizabeth were on hand for the opening of the St. Lawrence Seaway in 1959.

Today tourists can travel by barge boat on the Erie Canal.

The days of the Erie Canal as a key transportation route were over.

Today, the canal is used mostly by recreational boats. In 2001, it was designated a National Heritage Corridor. Visitors can still travel parts of the original canal. They can see the impressive series of locks at Lockport move boats up and down the steep Niagara Escarpment. They can admire the beautiful archways formed by old aqueducts crossing the rivers of New York. These aqueducts still stand as reminders of the time when "Clinton's Ditch" helped the nation grow.

GLOSSARY

berm—shoulder or ledge along a road or canal; the Erie Canal's berm measured 10 feet (3 meters) wide

cargo—the goods carried in a ship

escarpment—a long, steep ridge of land

locks—the parts of a canal into which water can be pumped in or out for lifting and lowering boats from one water level to another

packet boats—vessels that carry mail, passengers, and goods on a regular schedule

rapids—part of a river where the water flows very fast

seaboard—land bordering an ocean or sea

sluice—a narrow channel in a wall or gate that allows water to pass through

DID YOU KNOW?

- The ceremony in which De Witt Clinton poured water from Lake Erie into the Atlantic Ocean was called the Wedding of the Waters.

- Repairs to the canal were performed by workers in "hurry-up boats" who would speed to the scene of a problem.

- Packet boats carrying passengers down the canal often featured entertainment such as music, dancing, and games.

- Families who lived on canal boats kept their young children in harnesses attached to the boat by a rope. If the child fell overboard, he or she could be easily pulled back in.

IMPORTANT DATES

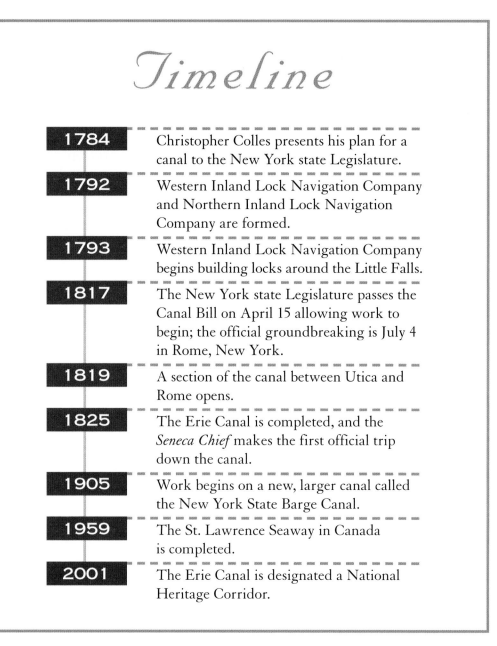

Timeline

1784 — Christopher Colles presents his plan for a canal to the New York state Legislature.

1792 — Western Inland Lock Navigation Company and Northern Inland Lock Navigation Company are formed.

1793 — Western Inland Lock Navigation Company begins building locks around the Little Falls.

1817 — The New York state Legislature passes the Canal Bill on April 15 allowing work to begin; the official groundbreaking is July 4 in Rome, New York.

1819 — A section of the canal between Utica and Rome opens.

1825 — The Erie Canal is completed, and the *Seneca Chief* makes the first official trip down the canal.

1905 — Work begins on a new, larger canal called the New York State Barge Canal.

1959 — The St. Lawrence Seaway in Canada is completed.

2001 — The Erie Canal is designated a National Heritage Corridor.

IMPORTANT PEOPLE

DE WITT CLINTON (1769–1828)

New York politician and leader of the movement to build the Erie Canal; as governor of New York from 1817 to 1823 and from 1825 to 1828, he presided over the beginning of construction and the completion of the canal

JAMES GEDDES (1763–1838)

Self-taught engineer and surveyor who surveyed the route of the Erie Canal; he later served in the New York state Legislature and the U.S. House of Representatives

THOMAS JEFFERSON (1743–1826)

Statesman and third president of the United States who did not support the building of the Erie Canal

CANVASS WHITE (1790–1834)

Engineer on the canal who discovered a quick-drying cement that held fast underwater

WANT TO KNOW MORE?

At the Library

Doherty, Craig A., and Katherine M. Doherty. *The Erie Canal.*
Woodbridge, Conn.: Blackbirch Press, 1997.

Lourie, Peter. *Erie Canal: Canoeing America's Great Waterway.* Honesdale,
Pa.: Boyds Mills Press, 1997.

Silverman, Jerry. *Singing Our Way West: Songs and Stories of America's
Westward Expansion.* Brookfield, Conn.: Millbrook Press, 1998.

On the Web

For more information on the *Erie Canal,* use FactHound

to track down Web sites related to this book.

1. Go to *www.facthound.com*

2. Type in a search word related to this book
   or this book ID: 0756506794.

3. Click on the *Fetch It* button.

Your trusty FactHound will fetch the best Web sites for you!

On the Road

Erie Canal Museum

318 Erie Blvd. E.

Syracuse, NY 13202

315/471-0593

To visit a museum housed in an 1850 building that served as a weigh station for boats on the original Erie Canal

Erie Canal Village

5789 New London Road

Rome, NY 13440

888/374-3226

To visit an outdoor living history museum

Chittenango Landing Canal Boat Museum

7010 Lakeport Road

Chittenango, NY 13037

315/687-3801

To learn how Erie Canal boats were built and repaired

Erie Canal Park

5750 Devoe Road

Camillus, NY 13031

315/488-3409

To visit a replica of an 1856 Erie Canal store and other displays

47

INDEX

About the Author

Andrew Santella writes for magazines and newspapers, including *GQ* and the *New York Times Book Review*. He is the author of a number of books for young readers. He lives outside Chicago with his wife and son.